# Easy Classical Masterworks for Melodica

# Easy Classical Masterworks for Melodica

Music of Bach, Beethoven, Brahms, Handel, Haydn, Mozart, Schubert, Tchaikovsky, Vivaldi and Wagner

Easy Classical Masterworks for Melodica

© Easy Classical Masterworks

ISBN-13:978-1499174908
ISBN-10:149917490X

*Bach*
Bourrée, BWV 996 .................................................. 9
Gavotte II, BWV 808 .............................................. 10
Menuett, BWV Anh 114 ............................................ 11

*Beethoven*
Chorfantasie Op. 80 ............................................... 15
Für Elise, WoO 59 ................................................ 16
Ode an die Freude, Op. 125 ........................................ 17

*Brahms*
Ungarischen Tänze N° 5, WoO 1 .................................... 21
Poco allegretto 3. Sinfonie F-Dur, op. 90 ......................... 22
Guten Abend, gut' Nacht ........................................... 23

*Handel*
Sarabande, HWV 437 ............................................... 27
Hallelujah, HWV 56 ............................................... 28
Water Music, HWV 349 ............................................. 29

*Haydn*
Sinfonie Nr. 94 G-Dur, Hob.I:94 .................................. 33

*Mozart*
"Ah vous dirais-je, Maman", K. 265 ............................... 37
Rondo Alla Turca, K. 331 ......................................... 38
40. Sinfonie, K.550 .............................................. 39

*Schubert*
Ständchen, D.957 ................................................. 43

*Tchaikovsky*
Dance of the Sugar Plum Fairy, Op. 71a ........................... 47
March, Op. 71a ................................................... 48
Sleeping Beauty Waltz, Op.66a .................................... 49

*Vivaldi*
la Primavera, RV. 269 ............................................ 53
l'Estate, RV. 315 ................................................ 54
l'Autunno, RV. 293 ............................................... 55
l'Inverno, RV. 297 ............................................... 56

*Wagner*
Tannhäuser Ouvertüre, WWV 70 ..................................... 59

# Bourrée, BWV 996

Johann Sebastian Bach

**Moderato**

# Gavotte II, BWV 808

Johann Sebastian Bach

**Andante**

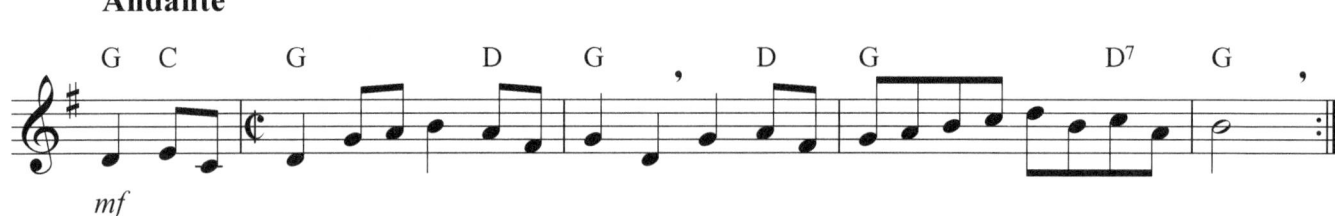

# Menuett, BWV Anh 114

Johann Sebastian Bach

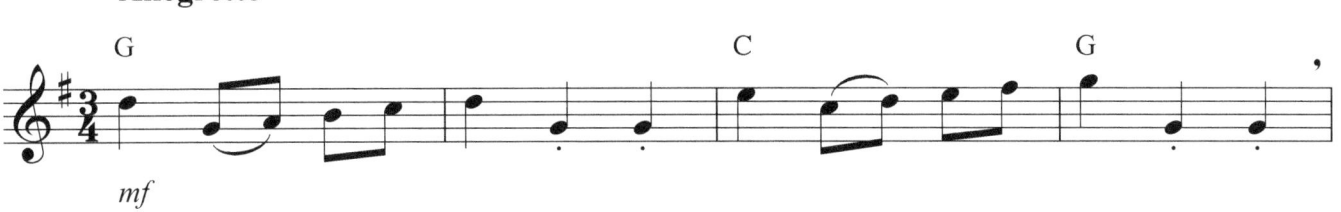

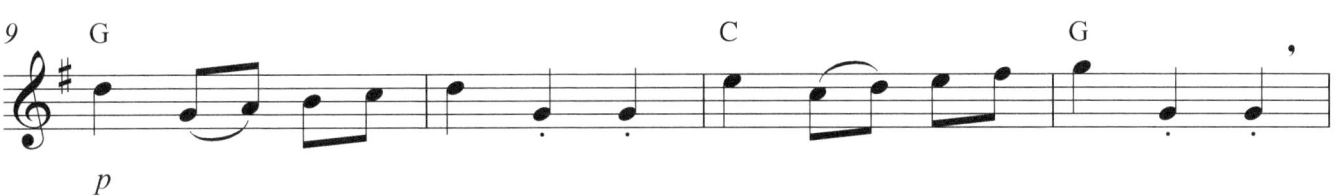

LUDWIG VAN BEETHOVEN

# Chorfantasie, Op. 80

Ludwig van Beethoven

# Für Elise, WoO 59

Ludwig van Beethoven

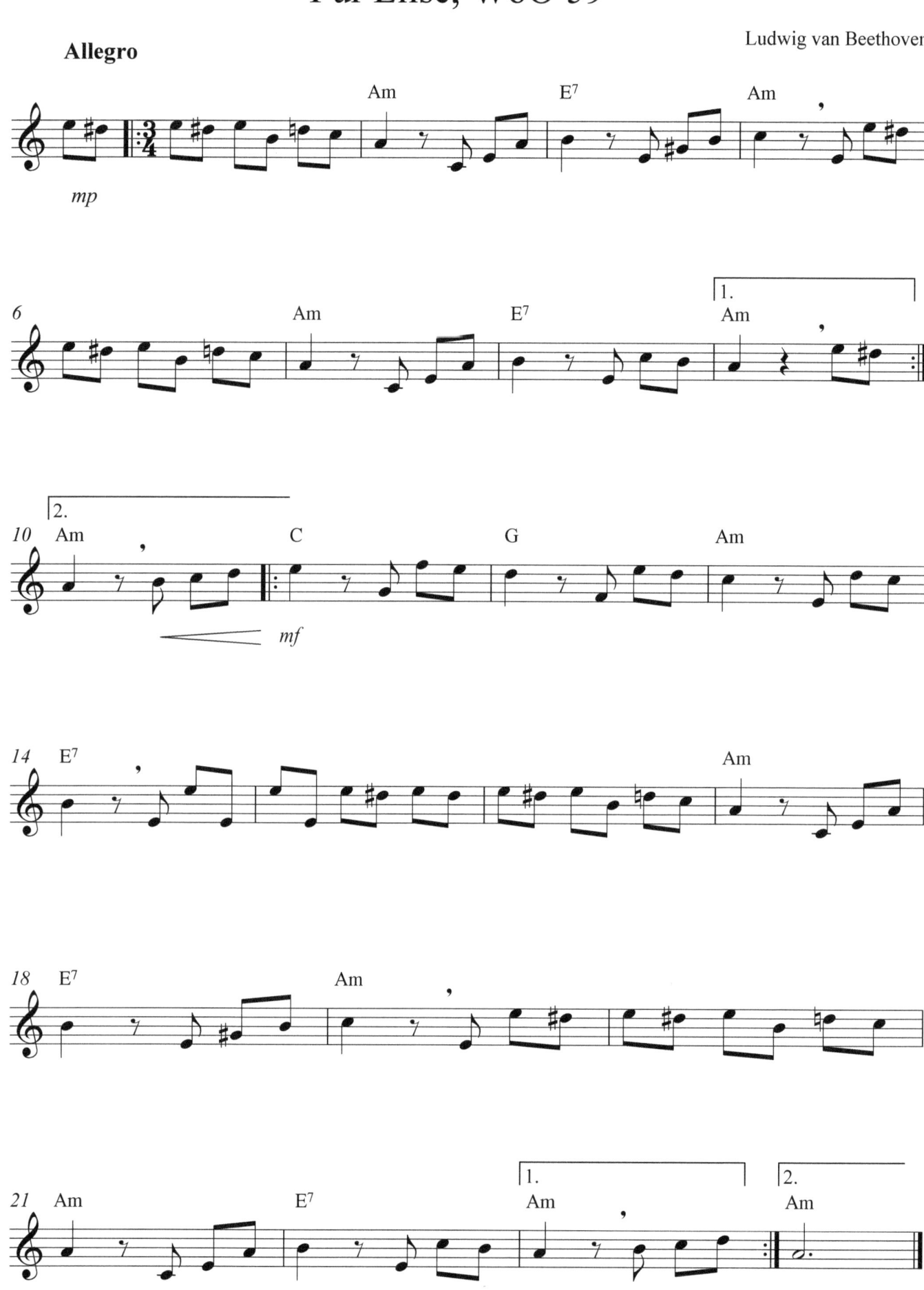

# Ode an die Freude, Op. 125

Ludwig van Beethoven

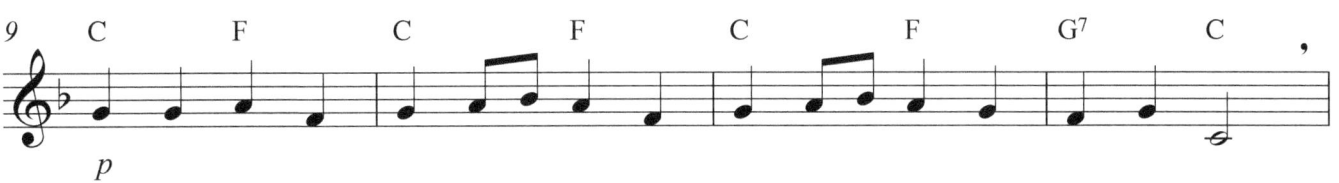

JOHANNES BRAHMS

# Ungarischen Tänze Nº 5, WoO 1

Johannes Brahms

# 3. Sinfonie F-Dur, op. 90

Johannes Brahms

**Poco allegretto**

# Guten Abend, gut' Nacht

Johannes Brahms

**Adagio**

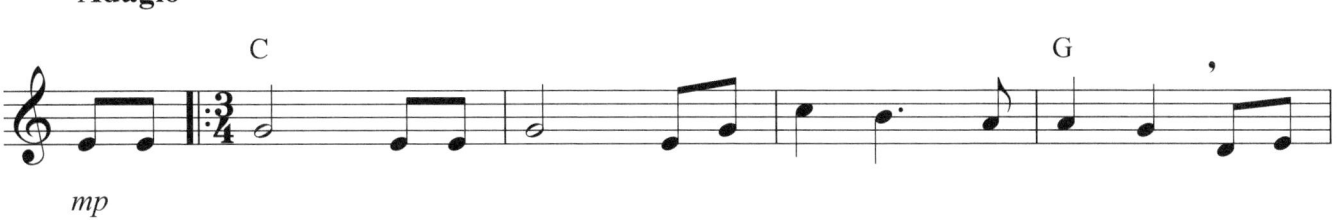

GEORGE HAENDEL

# Sarabande, HWV 437

George Frideric Handel

# Hallelujah, HWV 56

George Frideric Handel

**Allegro**

# Water Music, HWV 349

George Frideric Handel

**Alla Hornpipe**

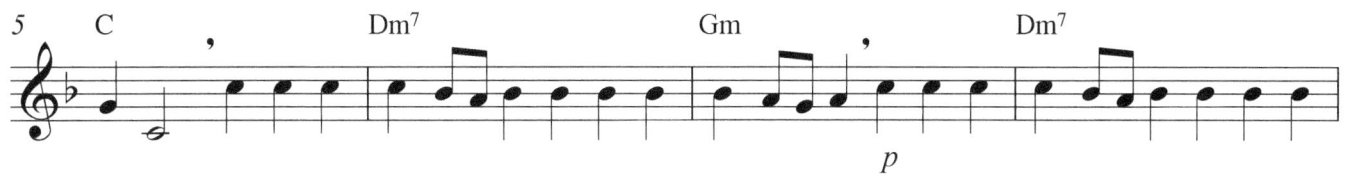
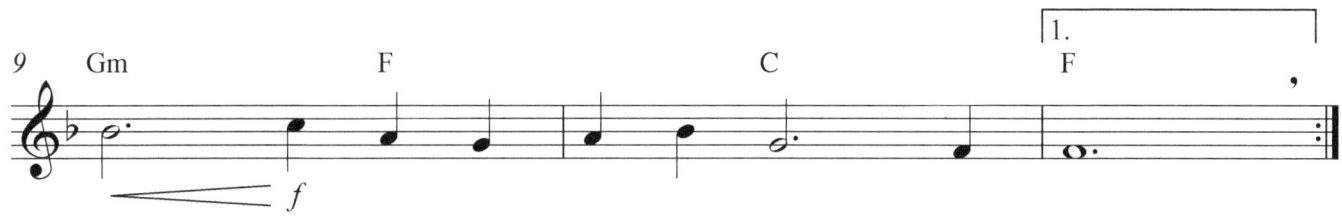

JOSEPH HAYON

# Sinfonie Nr. 94 G-Dur, Hob.I:94
"mit dem Paukenschlag"

Joseph Haydn

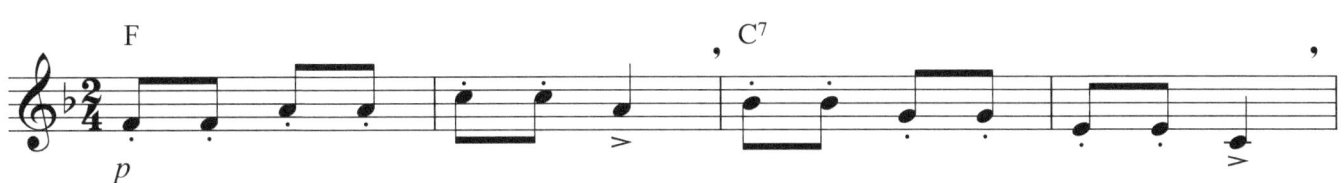
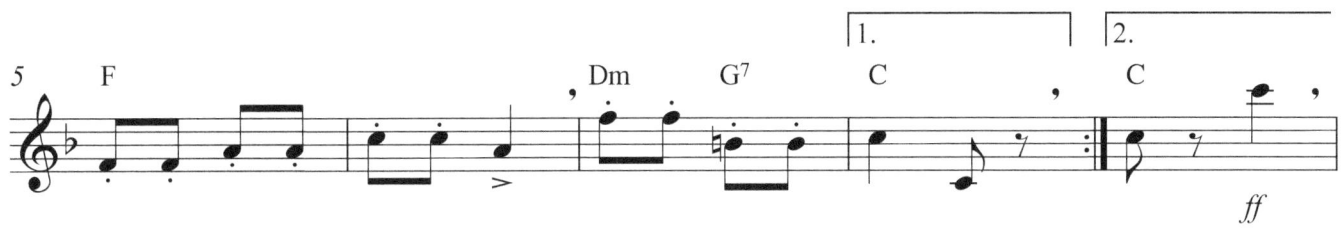

# Ah vous dirais-je, Maman

Wolfgang Amadeus Mozart

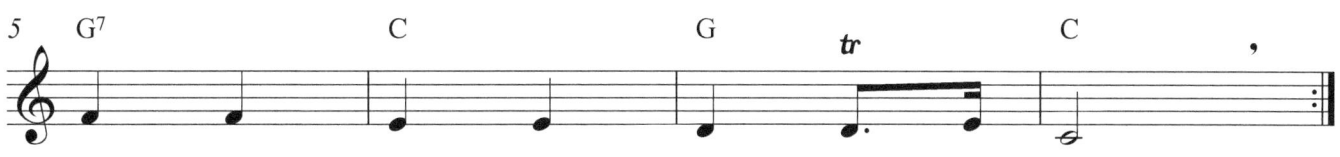

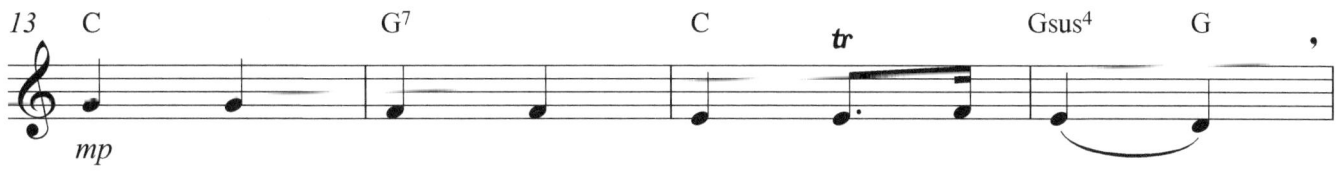
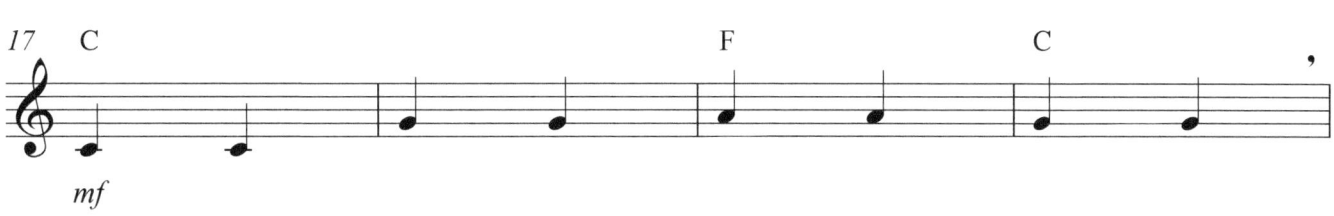
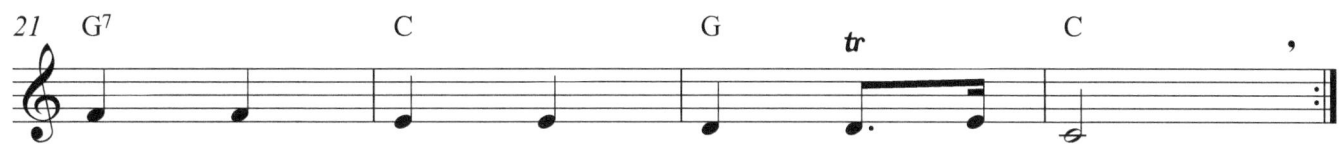

# Rondo Alla Turca, K. 331

Wolfgang Amadeus Mozart

**Allegro**

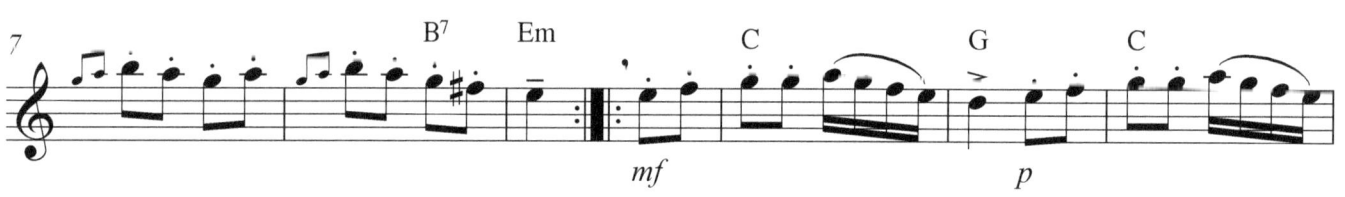

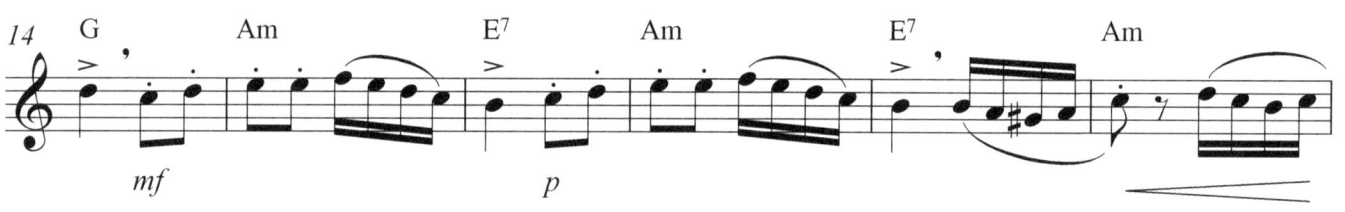

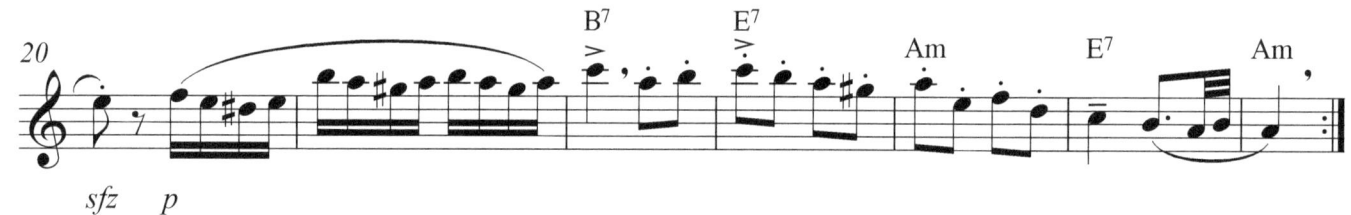

# 40. Sinfonie, K.550

Wolfgang Amadeus Mozart

**Allegro molto**

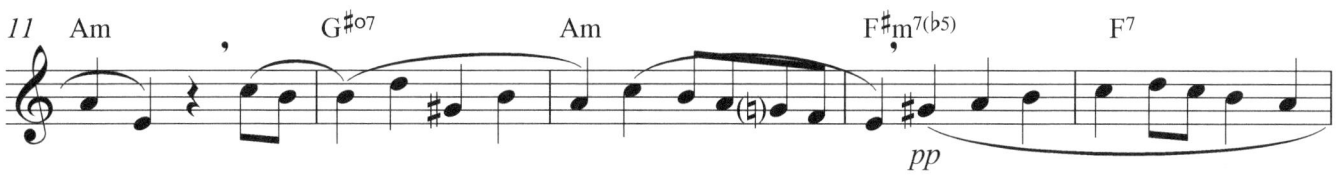

# Ständchen, D.957

Franz Schubert

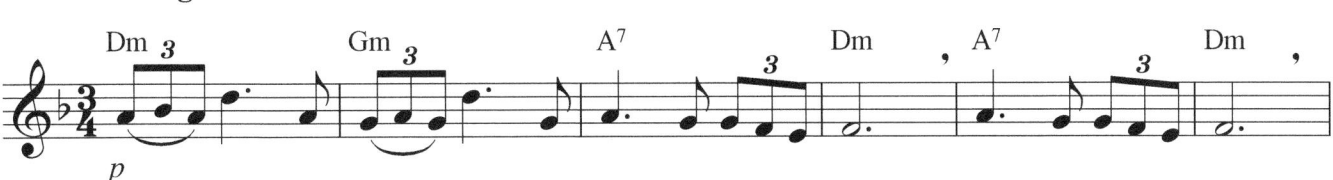

# Щелкунчик, Op. 71a

(Dance of the Sugar Plum Fairy)

Piotr Ilyich Tchaikovsky

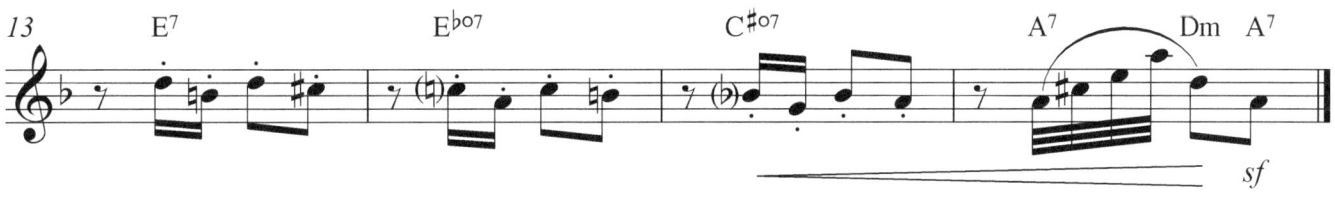

# Щелкунчик, Op. 71a

(March of The Nutcracker)

Piotr Ilyich Tchaikovsky

**Tempo di marcia**

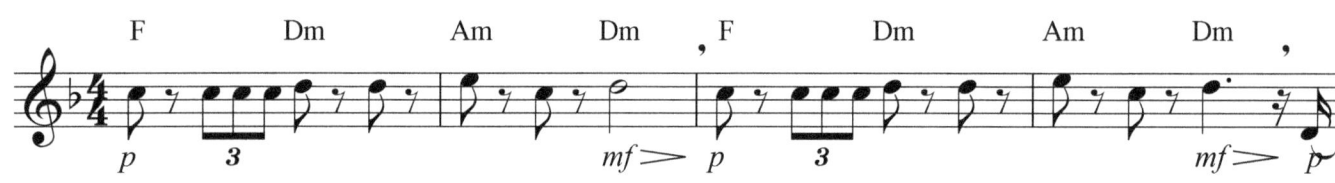

# Спящая красавица, Op.66а

(Sleeping Beauty Waltz)

Piotr Ilyich Tchaikovsky

**Allegro (tempo di valse)**

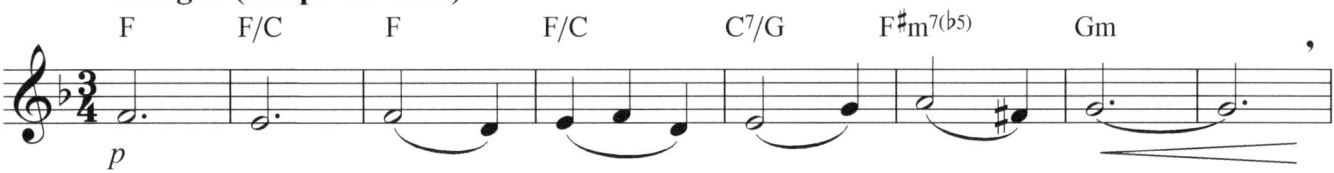

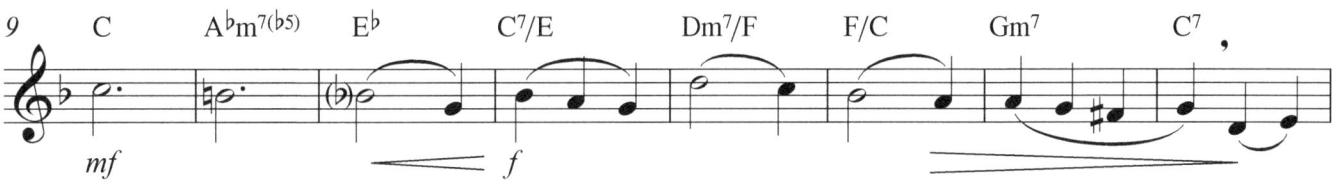

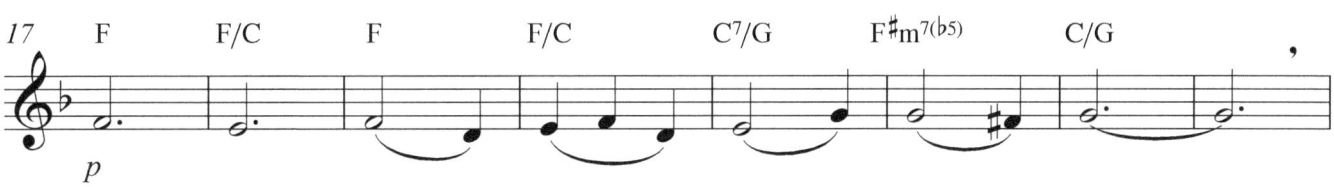

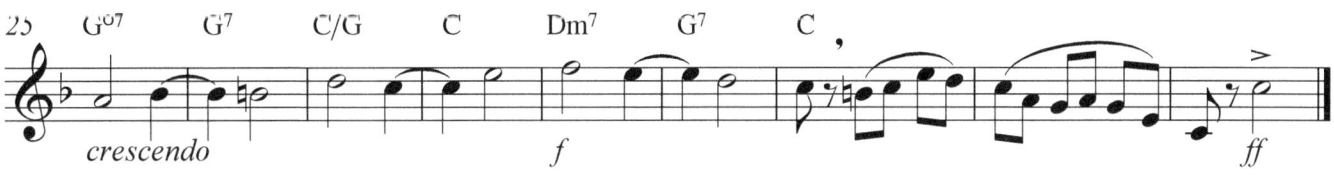

# la Primavera, RV. 269

Antonio Vivaldi

**Moderato**

# l'Estate, RV. 315

Antonio Vivaldi

**Allegro non molto**

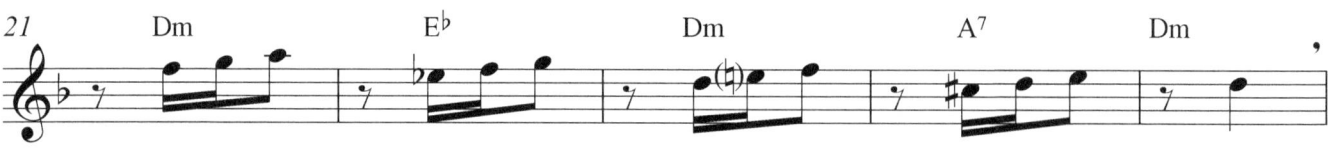

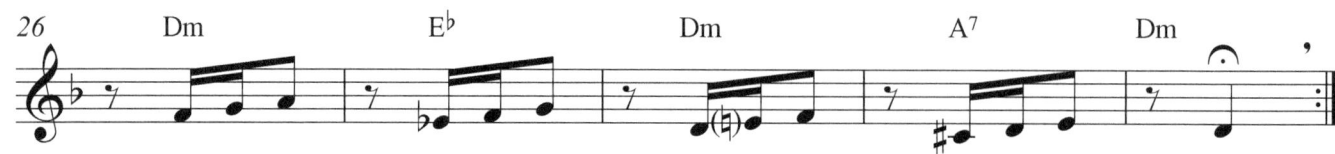

# l'Autunno, RV. 293

Antonio Vivaldi

# l'Inverno, RV. 297

Antonio Vivaldi

**Largo**

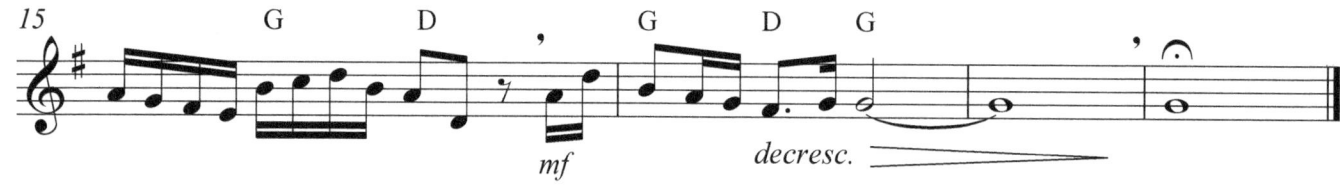

RICHARD WAGNER

# Tannhäuser Ouvertüre, WWV 70

Richard Wagner

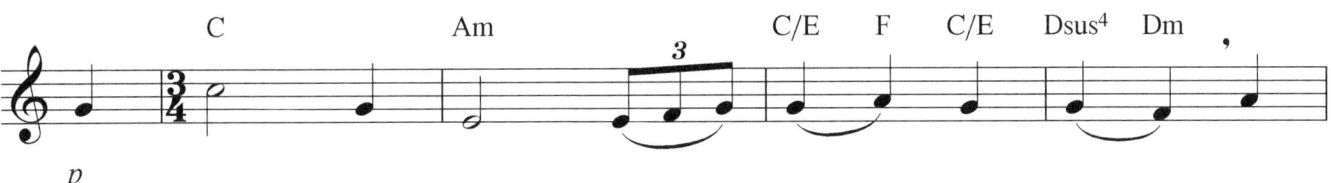
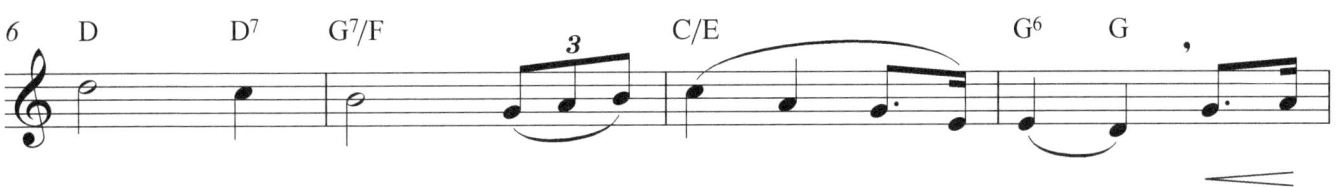
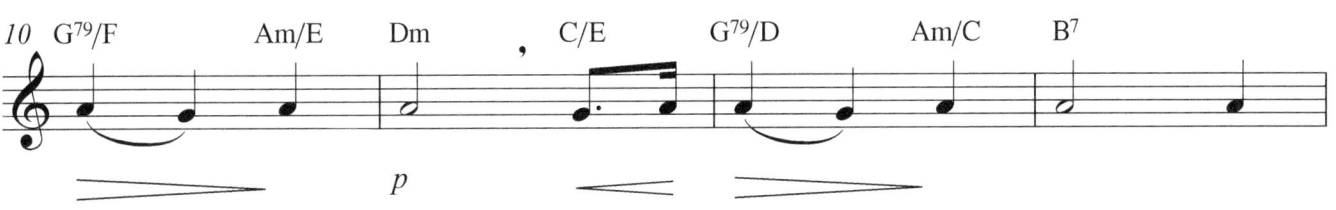
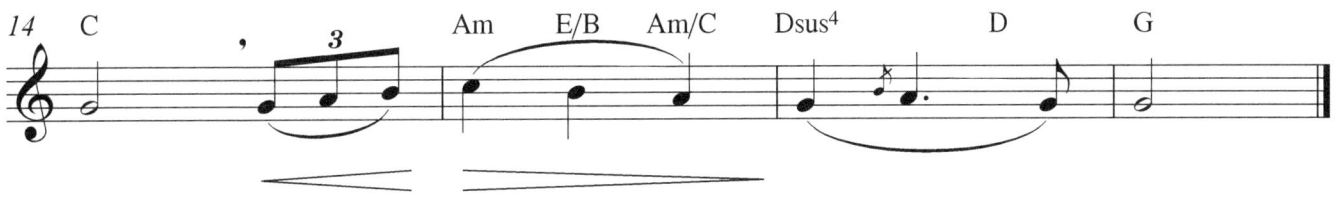

CPSIA information can be obtained
at www.ICGtesting.com
Printed in the USA
BVHW010222111218
535319BV00018B/470/P